YOU WERE BORN ON A ROTTEN DAY

By Jim Critchfield and Jerry Hopkins

Illustrated by ED POWERS

PRICE / STERN / SLOAN
Publishers, Inc., Los Angeles

TWELFTH PRINTING - JANUARY 1978

CAPRICORN

(December 22 — January 19)

CAPRICORN

People born under the sign of Capricorn make excellent cheapskates. If you were born on the 18th, you are one day older than people born on the 19th—but it doesn't matter because you're all cheapskates anyway.

Your love life is governed by the distant Planet Fringus (which is only three inches in diameter), and you have a tendency to be shy when undressing outdoors.

You must fight your primary weakness—delusions of adequacy, although with concentration and dedication you

could almost become
average. But never forget
you're a sub-standard
person.

Financial matters with
Capricorns are always
lousy, and you are unlucky
at love and finding water.
This birth sign is a
veritable hex, histori-
cally filled with gangsters,
misfits, perverts and TV
repairmen. Your general
health will continue to
deteriorate and you
probably won't make it
to the next full moon.
Always be of good cheer.

A TYPICAL MISERABLE CAPRICORN MONTH

1 This will be a memorable month — no matter how hard you try to forget it.

2 Leo is in your First House. Don't tell mate.

3 Afternoon very favorable for romance. Try a single person for a change.

4 Beware of low-flying butterflies.

5 Green light in A.M. for new projects. Red light in P.M. for traffic tickets.

6 Stars say fine for household chores. (They would! They all have hired help.)

7 You have just gone through a phase of great anxiety. Expect more of same.

8 Artistic ventures highlighted. Rob a museum.

9 Keep emotionally active. Cater to your favorite neurosis.

10 You will become a movie star before morning.

11 See your doctor without fail today. (Hang around the golf course, if necessary.)

12 Good day to buy a giraffe.

13 Buy another giraffe. The first one's getting lonely.

14 Fine day for romance with opposite sex (if that's your hangup).

15 A 1,000 pound safe will not fall on you today. Tomorrow, watch out.

16 Hate a loved one, but only in the P.M.

17 Help a swallow land at Capistrano.

18 Good time to do something flippant. Toss a few coins in the air.

19 Avoid gunfire in bathroom tonight.

20 Don't plan any hasty moves. You'll be evicted soon anyway.

21 Face facts concerning domestic situation. Ugh!

22 Your personal relationships are suffering. Good time to consider being a hermit.

23 Don't eat any poisonous foods in early A.M.

24 Touch a Playboy bunny tonight.

25 Prepare for a surprise.

26 Prepare for a disappointment.

27 Keep preparing. Something's bound to happen.

28 Half Moon tonight. (But it's better than no Moon at all).

29 Another good night not to sleep in a eucalyptus tree.

30 Message will arrive in the mail today. Destroy, before the FBI sees it.

ARIES

(March 21 — April 20)

ARIES

If you are an Aries, you are probably lonely — and with your personality it's no wonder. Although the Aries-born do become attached to others, the others rarely become attached to them. So, if you're an Aries, it's best to take up single games at an early age, like solitaire and mugging.

Aries men and women are adversely affected by the moon, often baying at it and searching for Grunion on the wrong night. And when people of other signs are making love under the harvest moon, some Aries nut will be out in the middle of

the freeway trying to
shuck wheat.

Aries people are also
quick to grasp any
opportunity, and any-
thing else that's lying
around loose. Fortified
with a keen memory and
a cheap camera, many excel
at blackmail.

These Ram-born people
appreciate being looked up
to and often saw the legs
off other people's chairs.
If this sign rules you,
your lucky color is not
as good as it used to be,
your Lucky Day is Doris,
your Lucky Star hasn't
made a picture since 1917
and famous people born
in this sign are not very
famous.

A TYPICAL MISERABLE ARIES MONTH

1 This is your day! FORGET IT!

2 Do what comes naturally now. Seethe and fume and throw a tantrum.

3 Stars indicate need for authority. Talk to an FBI man soon.

4 Good day for business affairs. Make a pass at the new file clerk.

5 You may get an opportunity for advancement today. What a joke!

6 Perfect day for scrubbing the floor and other exciting things.

7 You will buy a used bird cage before midnight.

8 Be free and open and breezy! Enjoy! Things won't get any better so get used to it.

9 Truth will out this morning. (Which may really mess things up.)

10 Tonight's the night. Sleep in a eucalyptus tree.

11 Fine day to get rid of old inventory. Sell the Zeppelin.

12 There may be troubled waters in the A.M. Call the plumber.

13 Travel important today; Internal Revenue men arrive tomorrow.

14 Stars in conflict today. For details see Six O'clock News.

15 Good day for a change of scene. Repaper the bedroom wall.

16 You can create your own opportunities this week. Blackmail a senior executive.

17

18 Yesterday was a blank, wasn't it?

19 Mate will need pat on the back today. Probably a chicken bone in her throat.

20 Fine day to throw a party. Throw him as far as you can.

21 Good news. Ten weeks from Friday will be a pretty good day.

22 If you find a lost python today, be sure and return it to owner.

23 Lie about something important today.

24 Think of your family tonight. Try to crawl home after the bar closes.

25 Good time to think about money. Follow a Brinks' truck for a while.

26 Show respect for age. Drink good Scotch for a change.

27 Give thought to your reputation. Consider changing name and moving to a new town.

28 Surprising event linked with close kin. A relative is about to borrow money.

29 Future seems cloudy. Buy new raincoat.

30 If you think last Tuesday was a drag, wait till you see what happens tomorrow!

TAURUS

(April 21 – May 20)

TAURUS

The Taurean is warmth
and soft lights and love.
Aphrodite was a Taurus,
and she had a perfume
named after her — so keep
on the lookout for a
good side deal.

Men and women born
under this sign are
known in the Zodiacal
spheres as "The Silent
Ones." No loud talkers
here. No college orators.
No loud-mouths. But it's
mainly because they have
nothing to say. In spite of
this, they usually manage
to destroy an interesting
conversation.

Because they prefer
quiet, hushed work,
many Taurus people

have gone on to become internationally famous counterfeiters, pickpockets and grave robbers. And because they are so quiet, their appearance is extremely important. So if you are a Taurus, for God's sake do something about your shoes.

Taurus ladies make wonderful wives as they have an underdeveloped ability to nag in the traditional American manner. This is because they usually have their mouths filled with their husbands' fists. Your birthstone is plastic and your Lucky Color is puce. Your Lucky Day is Dennis, and your Lucky Number is MCXXVII.

A TYPICAL MISERABLE
TAURUS MONTH

1 Excellent day to have a rotten day.

2 Fly to work this morning.

3 Do not drink to excess today. But you *can* arink to anything else you like.

4 Say "Hello" to a crocus.

5 You worry too much about your job. Stop it. You are not paid enough to worry.

6 Get old problems out of the way. File for divorce.

7 Don't tell any big lies today. Small ones can be just as effective.

8 Others will look to you for stability; so hide when you bite your nails.

9 Keep your eyes on possessions today. And keep your hands to yourself.

10 Don't let your imagination run away with you. People really *are* talking behind your back.

11 Let the Aries out of someone's tires. Ho, Ho, Ho. (That's a big Astrology "in" joke.)

12 Evening hours "all clear" for romance. Tell mate you have to work late.

13 Bad day for giraffes.

14 For you who have an Oedipus complex, cool it.

15 Take a little jaunt today. (A large jaunt if nobody's looking.)

16 You are one day older than yesterday.

17 Don't marry a longshoreman or woman in the A.M.

18 Beware of your best friends in early P.M. They are the worst people in the world.

19 Guard against offending anyone during this period. Use a man's deodorant.

20 Excellent day for drinking heavily. Spike office water cooler.

21 Good time for colossal undertaking. Take a giant to lunch.

22 Don't overexert yourself. You've done nothing for so long it might be fatal.

23 Early morning hours will be good for shearing sheep.

24 Excellent time to become a missing person.

25 You will be alone today. Spend free time feeling sorry for person you love best . . . you.

26 Don't wear a bikini to work today.

27 Be sociable. Speak to the person next to you in the unemployment line.

28 Libra rising. You stay in bed.

29 A run-away box-kite will get you today.

30 A day for firm decisions!!!!! Or is it?

GEMINI

(May 21 – June 21)

GEMINI

Castor and Pollux
represent the twins of
Gemini and neither
should be taken on an
empty stomach. Persons
born under this
sign are never what
they appear to be. The
Gemini-born love to
"strike a pose," which
is fine as long as the
blinds are pulled and
you're positive neither
of the girls is a
vice cop.

If you are a Gemini,
you are a "natural" for
show biz. You wear
lamp shades at parties,
clean out elephant barns,
and dance a dirty
quadrille.

You attract attention
naturally because of your

tendency to carry tubas
on subways and crowded
elevators, and to challenge
people to Indian wrestling
matches. Because you
are such a so-so actor,
your chances in politics
are excellent.

Pluto and Neptune, the
planets which are bad
news everywhere, are
your planets, making you
irresponsible, incorrigible,
unmanageable and fun
to be with.

You do not believe in the
accurate, proven, time-
tested predictions of
horoscopes. Thus, most
astrologers can't stand
you any more than your
relatives can. Your Lucky
Star is Lassie and you
obviously have no Lucky
Number at all.

A TYPICAL MISERABLE
GEMINI MONTH

1 This month will be truly wonderful. But not for you.

2 Give your talent the room it requires. Perhaps the bedroom?

3 Do NOT read your horoscope today.

4 Fine time to bury the hatchet. But after dark and no witnesses.

5 A Capricorn will proposition you soon. Get paid first.

6 O.K. to go along with family wishes. Move out.

7 You will receive something to have and to hold . . . a baby with a wet diaper.

8 Emphasis is on love and marriage, but not with the same person.

9 Your life is a bed of roses today. Watch out for the arsenic spray.

10 A tipsy Playboy bunny will enter your life in the late P.M.

11 Expect some incredible luck . . . like picking a shopping cart with four good wheels.

12 Get plenty of rest this evening. Quarrel with spouse at dinner.

13 Today you will think you're at wit's end. Not so. Your wit ended two years ago.

14 Don't play the bagpipes before noon today.

15 If you are over 6'8", give some thought to renting yourself out as a flagpole.

16 Surprise in store concerning partnership. He's found out what you're doing.

17 Beware of high-handedness today. Don't pet giraffes.

18 Stellar rays say protect all precious possessions. Bury trading stamps at once.

19 Accent is on career. Keep at least one iron in the fire. And take a toaster to bed.

20 Fine day to work off excess energy. Steal something heavy.

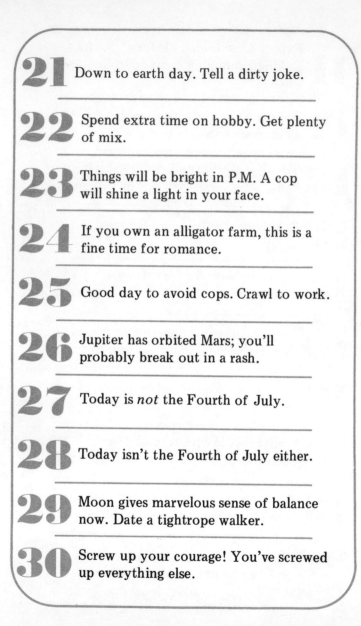

21 Down to earth day. Tell a dirty joke.

22 Spend extra time on hobby. Get plenty of mix.

23 Things will be bright in P.M. A cop will shine a light in your face.

24 If you own an alligator farm, this is a fine time for romance.

25 Good day to avoid cops. Crawl to work.

26 Jupiter has orbited Mars; you'll probably break out in a rash.

27 Today is *not* the Fourth of July.

28 Today isn't the Fourth of July either.

29 Moon gives marvelous sense of balance now. Date a tightrope walker.

30 Screw up your courage! You've screwed up everything else.

CANCER

(June 22 – July 22)

CANCER

Individuals born under this sign are outstanding in crafts that require painstaking, careful handiwork. The men are especially good at knitting booties and the women very creative at welding and fixing faulty plumbing fixtures.

Cancer people are the "chosen ones" of the Zodiac, lucky in love, good-natured, terribly, terribly fat and ill-mannered.

If you are a Cancer, you will find great happiness with anyone, anywhere, at any time, doing anything. Conversely, however,

marrying another Cancer
is not recommended
since moon children
are usually out of work
and you'd both starve
to death.

The retentive mental
powers of people born
in this sphere are over-
developed. You undoubt-
edly remember every
dirty joke you ever
heard and among your
friends you are considered
a classic bore. You can
succeed at anything
if you compete against
small stupid children and
people with great handi-
caps.

Your Lucky Day was
May 3, 1851. Your Lucky
Color runs when laundered
in hot water, and
about half of you
think you're women.

A TYPICAL MISERABLE
CANCER MONTH

1 Increased knowledge will help you now.
Have mate's phone bugged.

2 Stellar rays prove fibbing never pays.
Embezzlement is another matter.

3 Don't believe everything you hear or
anything you say.

4 Do something unusual today. Pay a bill.

5 You will be a winner today. Pick a
fight with a four-year-old.

6 Time to take stock. Go home with some
office supplies.

7 Quiet day. Loud night. Police will
break up party by 2 A.M.

8 Romance is moving by leaps and bounds.
You are in love with a kangaroo.

9 Make friendships more lasting. Seal
someone in plastic.

10 Kitchen activity is highlighted. Butter
up a friend.

11 Excellent day for money matters. Forge a check before lunch.

12 Practice temperance this week. Water mate's drinks.

13 Be more aggressive. Apply for welfare.

14 Absence of lunar vibrations. Call masseur.

15 You have been bitchy since Tuesday and you'll probably get fired today.

16 Advice to women under Leo: Careful.

17 Don't play the organ tonight.

18 Good day for water sports. Take a bath with a friend.

19 Dreary morning, boring afternoon, quarrelsome evening. Avoid razor blades.

20 Stay away from bicycle chains.

21 Venus is now astrologically square with Pluto. That means there isn't a hip planet left.

22 Lyrical day. Family harmonious. (But piano may be a little flat.)

23 Troubled day for virgins over 16 who are beautiful and wealthy and live in eucalyptus trees.

24 Give way to normal tendencies. Be hateful and boring.

25 Don't wear your heart on your sleeve. That campy wristwatch is already making people stare.

26 The love of your life may appear in A.M. (Act as though you recognize her in daylight.)

27 Be leery of Scorpios with migraines.

28 Another sparkling day! Probably Burgundy.

29 Seek spiritual insight. Visit a friend at the Midnight Mission.

30 Don't play hopscotch before 6 A.M.

LEO

(July 23 — August 22)

LEO

The Leo-born are often thought to be sentimental. This is not true. They are actually crybabies. You can identify a Leo by finding a person who is sucking his thumb and telling everyone how poor he is. If you sympathize with him he cries because he thinks you agree; if you don't, he cries louder because you are such an insensitive person.

But Leos are very giving — always ready to give others bad advice and a hard time. The most famous person born under this sign was Herman W. Mobley,

and there have been
so few others that
many hospitals are no
longer recording births
during this cycle. Leos
can find a happy solution
for their problems:
Usually it's four parts
gin to one part
vermouth. Many Leos
end up in jail,
either as prisoners
or guards.

If you are a Leo,
your Lucky Day is Dooms,
your birthstone is mud,
and you suffer from an
annoying affliction you
contracted at a small
intimate party.

A TYPICAL MISERABLE
LEO MONTH

1 Don't abandon hope. Your Captain Midnight decoder ring arrives tomorrow.

 Lavish spending can be disastrous. Don't buy any lavishes for a while.

 Good time to excel in home-wrecking.

 Excellent day for taking out insurance on a friend who isn't feeling well.

 Beware of strangers bearing used soda straws.

 Think about Charlton Heston today.

 Take it easy in P.M., especially with mate (or Chief Petty Officer, if he drops over first).

 Lady Luck brings added income today. Lady friend takes it away tonight.

9 Do something stupid again today.

10 Venus adversely configured. Probably something she ate.

11 Excellent day to test your luck. Call your mother-in-law.

12 Surprise due today. Also the rent.

13 Good day to go moose-hunting with a belly-dancer.

14 Venus is moving into a new sector. Good riddance.

15 Slow day. Practice crawling.

16 Spread some sunshine today. It's silly — but it keeps you out of the pool hall.

17 Accent is on the bedroom tonight. Too bad you'll have a splitting headache.

18 Watch the sunrise this morning. But go to bed first.

19 Start the day with a smile. After that you can be your nasty old self again.

20 Time to be aggressive. Go after a tattooed Virgo.

21 Be sure to keep beauty appointment. You can't afford to miss one.

22 Don't paint the sidewalk today.

23 Be prepared to accept sacrifices. Vestal virgins aren't all that bad.

24 Day of surprises. Your best friend is about to do you-know-what with you-know-who.

25 Avoid reality at all costs.

26 Don't cheat anyone before noon.

27 If your mother was a Virgo, lots of luck!

28 You will buy a medieval castle by dusk.

29 Good night to spend with family. But avoid arguments with your mate's new lover.

30 Excellent lunar rays will bring change. And will it be awful!

VIRGO

(August 23 – September 23)

VIRGO

Virgo is the peppiest of the Signs. The Virgo is extremely talented, quick to absorb facts and free food. The need to express himself creatively is instinctive. It was a Virgo who first got the idea to engrave the Lord's Prayer on the head of a friend.

It was a Virgo who invented a garbage can with remote control, so you can change garbage from wherever you're sitting.

Due to the influence of the Virginal aspects of this sign, chastity, purity and cleanliness are permanent, damaging hang-ups. Financial problems can also arise here, so Virgos often leave

a standing order with the
courts for one bankruptcy
a year. The chances are the
last panhandler you avoided
was a Virgo genius who's
been down on his luck
for 37 years.

If you are a Virgo, it would
not be a bad idea to start
speaking softly and carry a
bail-bondsman's phone number.
A lot of people are out to get
you. Your Lucky Number has
been disconnected, your Lucky
Break will probably be your
arm, and the Good Fairy who
watches over you has just
been arrested.

A TYPICAL MISERABLE VIRGO MONTH

1 Emphasis is on deep romance. Take your date to a mine shaft.

2 Don't plant potatoes today.

3 Good day to let down old friends who need help.

4 Practice thrift this week. Stop over-tipping the garbage man.

5 Take your Senator to lunch this week.

6 If you are under three feet tall, avoid four-foot snow drifts for a while.

7 Good day to have a bad day.

8 Forget about revenge today. Wait until tomorrow.

9 Desires are not necessarily needs. Take lots of cold showers.

10

11 Ignore yesterday's horoscope; also ignore tomorrow's horoscope.

12

13 Good time to swim the English Channel.

14 Next Thursday will not be your lucky day.

15 Next Friday will not be your lucky day. As a matter of fact, you don't have a lucky day this year.

16 Timing must be perfect now. Two-timing must be better than perfect.

17 Make every effort to get to the heart of the matter. Take somebody's pulse tonight.

18 The Moon is blue. And Jupiter's not too happy either.

19 Accent on helpful side of your nature. Drain the moat.

20 Put your best foot forward. Or just call in and say you're sick.

21 You will probably feel devilish tonight. Throw a dynamite cap under a Flamenco dancer's heels.

22 Glorious day for socializing in swank spot. Too bad you can't afford it.

23 Be more friendly. Smile when you get today's traffic ticket.

24 You are a tower of strength in the office, but only so-so in bed.

25 Go to church today. Pray for surf.

26 Good day for casual remarks. Talk about 1967.

27 Perfect time for marriage. If you're married, perfect time for divorce.

28 Don't milk any goats under water today.

29 Partying is okay, but how long can you keep going without sleep?

30 You'll soon heave a sigh of relief. And with your luck, it will heave you back.

LIBRA

Libra is the marriage
sign. Librans possess
cheerful dispositions,
generally attracting mem-
bers of the opposite sex,
and, occasionally, some
of the same sex. But no
matter.

Cuddlesomeness and
warmth abound in
Librans. The only real
problem is that they
never know when to
stop. A Libran will
keep on being cheerful
and attractive to
others forever, tending
to remarry often, with
or without legal
sanction. Life is one
big tacit wedding vow
after another.

If your wife is a
Libran, it is suggested
that you buy your milk
at the store, burn wood
so no one comes to read
the gas meter, and if
you have a best friend,
shoot him since it's a
cinch something is
going on.

If your husband is a
Libran, get a job and
let him stay home with
the kids because once
he steps out the front
door, it's "So Long,
Charlie!"

Your Lucky Number is
on a house somewhere, your
Lucky Star wears falsies,
your Lucky Planet is a
geranium and your
Lucky Word is "No."

A TYPICAL MISERABLE
LIBRA MONTH

 1 A good day to accept the inevitable. You're a loser — you might as well face it.

2 Early afternoon could be troublesome. And you are the cause of it all.

3 You must face reality. Dustin Hoffman is not in love with you.

 4 Good day for flying. Bad day for landing.

 5 Think big. Pollute the Mississippi.

6 You are wise, witty and wonderful, but you spend too much time reading this sort of stuff.

7 Watch out for talkative nudists in early A.M.

8 Bad time to increase production. Avoid mate.

9 Good day to deal with people in high places. Particularly lonely stewardesses.

 10 What the hell, go ahead and put all your eggs in one basket.

11 A long-forgotten loved one will appear soon. Buy the negative at any price.

12 Ignore failure in P.M. Try again next A.M.

13 Don't eat any string today. Or tomorrow, for that matter.

14 Important to buy something expensive . . . . even if you pay for it yourself.

15 Paint a hockey puck plaid today.

16 Don't get up until you go to bed tomorrow.

17 You tend to be excessively hostile. Drop plot to overthrow City Council.

18 Fine time to please business associates. Resign.

19 Good period for being positive. Lead a horse to water (and insist that he drink).

20 Good day to make advances. Wink at someone.

21 Good time to help someone less fortunate than yourself, if there is anyone.

22 You are restless now and desirous of change. Try two dimes and a nickel.

23 You are one in a million, and the other 999,999 sure aren't too happy about it!

24 You're a person everyone confides in. Too bad you're such a gossip.

25 Think a dirty thought before lunch. Maybe even before breakfast.

26 If you're a sailor, you will befriend a wounded dolphin this week.

27 Make headway at work. Continue to let things deteriorate at home.

28 You always look for the sunny side of things. Anything to save on the light bill.

29 Be helpful today, even if it upsets you to do it.

30 You were born to enjoy bliss. Unfortunately, she moved to Paris two years ago.

SCORPIO

(October 23 — November 21)

SCORPIO

Men and women born
under the Sign of Scorpio
have very active minds,
bodies, and police
records.

This sign is all fuzzed up
with mythological
happenings about a
pretty lady who gave a
nice man a scorpion
which promptly bit him
and gave him such a
lump he never got
over it.

Mercury rules ˙he pelvis
of each Scorpio. (You
can just imagine what
that causes when the
lights are out.) Due to
this pelvic problem,
the Scorpio has a thing
about love. Crying out
for love, but shoving it

away when it comes.
(Doesn't this one
choke you up?)
Scorpio women are very
giving by nature, which
always makes them
sought after by men who
throw big parties.
Scorpio men, on the
other hand, find happi-
ness in the Armed
Services, since they are
marvelous cheaters at
poker and craps. The
Scorpio-born should try
to direct their emotions
toward more healthy out-
lets . . . like organizing
waterfalls . . . or sending
gift packages to needy
CIA men.
If you are a Scorpio,
never play with your
yo-yo in public. Your
Lucky Color is fading,
and your Lucky Day is
worse than most.

A TYPICAL MISERABLE
SCORPIO MONTH

1 This month will be so bad you won't believe it.

2 You often take the wrong tack. Don't let the lady at the tie counter catch you.

3 If you're carrying a torch, put it down. The Olympics are over.

4 Questionable day. Ask somebody something.

5 Period of personal adjustment. Straighten seams.

6 Your inner conflicts may lead to heated argument . . . you little devil you!

7 You will receive an unusual foreign convertible. A '65 rickshaw.

8 Don't go surfing in South Dakota for a while.

9 Don't read any sky-writing for the next two weeks.

10 Wonderful day. Your hangover just makes it seem terrible.

11 Try to control your tendency to be repetitive. (Which is another way of saying you're a bore.)

12 Don't be taken off guard. You'd make a lousy fullback.

13 Wait for further instructions.

14 Venus crossed Jupiter. Some rumble to-night.

15 Slow down! Be cautious! Eat well. And stop standing on your head so much.

16 Celebrate Hannibal Day this year. Take an elephant to lunch.

17 Your positive attitude always enables you to see the seamy side of life.

18 Spotlight is on long range plans. Think about 1994 a lot.

19 Don't buy a trampoline from a Libra today.

20 Mix a one-to-one Martini for a friend you hate.

21 Don't dig sand crabs for the next 10 days.

22 People are beginning to notice you. Try dressing *before* you leave the house.

23 See! We told you not to dig sand crabs.

24 Picture not good. Adjust horizontal knob.

25 Remember a forgotten face today. Call mate.

26 Good time to change oil and religion.

27 Be independent. Insult a rich relative today.

28 You have a wonderful way with children, which gives people a pretty good clue to your emotional age.

29 Learn to hold your head high, or you'll get busted for being stoned.

30 Okay to dig sand crabs again.

SAGITTARIUS

(November 22 — December 21)

SAGITTARIUS

Sagittarians are represented by the Centaur — half man and half horse.

Naturally, this half-and-half symbol produces a dual personality, both parts equally unpleasant. The constant conflict keeps coming to the surface and prodding people who are impossible to get along with.

A Sagittarian would even have trouble making friends with a rubber tree. The nicest person born under this sign was Scrooge. Sagittarians are ruled by Jupiter, the planet of expansion, which

explains their love of
eating. They will eat
just about anything, and
too much of it. Let's
face it, Sagittarius,
you are a fat person.

But you are not with-
out hope. You sit
around hoping a lot,
wear wishing rings and
spend hours throwing
pennies into wells.

Your Compatible Sign
is "No Left Turn,"
your birthstone is fake,
your Lucky Number is
missing, and your
Lucky Star is having
a thing with her agent.

A TYPICAL MISERABLE
SAGITTARIUS MONTH

1 Don't go prospecting with a homicidal Scorpio today.

2 Stay out of burning buildings this afternoon.

3 Don't climb Mt. Everest with a Virgo today.

4 Good time to patronize your local taxidermist.

5 Your goose is cooked. And your current chick is burned up too.

6 Fine day for friends. Terrible day for you.

7 Dickering is out today. Dockering is O.K.

8 Stay away from hurricanes for a while.

9 You are all things to all men. If you're a lady and you're married, you may be in big trouble.

10 Explore new avenues to solve financial problems. Panhandle downtown for a change.

11 Mars influence may bring happy surprise. Then again it may not.

12 Try to advance career in evening. (Heaven knows, you're not having much luck in the daytime.)

13 Full moon highlights everything tonight. If you are a cat-burglar, wait a few days.

14 Day of comfort. Visit Davenport, Iowa.

15 Take everything in stride. Trample anyone who gets in your way.

16 Good time to buy an airline. If you're TWA, good time to sell one.

17 Be candid today. Insult a close friend.

18 Expect disappointment, pain, frustration, rejection. Favorable day for romance.

19 If office party runs late, put in for overtime.

20 Fine evening for Caroling. Or Phyllising. Or Esthering.

21 A chubby man with a white beard and a red suit will approach you soon. Avoid him. He's a Commie.

22 Spruce up for Spring! Have your feather boa cleaned.

23 Try a foreign entanglement. Kung Fu experts can be very romantic.

24 Stay out of bottomless pits for the rest of the year.

25 Watch out for cold wave this week. (Or maybe warm WAC.)

26 Good time to take long look at self. (But don't undress in public to do it.)

27 Day for good connection. Place long distance call to Nairobi.

28 A tall stranger wearing dark clothes will escort you to jail. Be pleasant.

29 Virgo is conjunct your ascendant today. And you know what that means!

30 Wait for further instructions.

pss!

This book is published by

PRICE/STERN/SLOAN
Publishers, Inc., Los Angeles

whose other splendid titles include such literary classics as:

ART AFTERPIECES ($2.95)

THE DISRESPECTFUL DICTIONARY ($2.50)

HOW TO BE AN ITALIAN ($2.50)

HOW TO BE A JEWISH MOTHER ($2.50)

LOVE IS ALWAYS LOSING AT TENNIS ($2.50)

NEVER SWEAR AT A CHRYSANTHEMUM ($2.50)

THE POWER OF POSITIVE PESSIMISM ($1.25)

THE VERY IMPORTANT PERSON NOTE BOOK ($2.50)

They are available wherever books are sold, or may be
ordered directly from the publisher by sending
check or money order for total amount plus 50 cents
(handling and mailing fee). For a complete list,
send a *stamped, self-addressed* envelope to:

PRICE/STERN/SLOAN
Publishers, Inc.
410 North La Cienega Boulevard
Los Angeles, California 90048